Riddle Me This!

Riddles at School

Lisa Regan

WINDMILL
BOOKS

NEW YORK

Published in 2015 by Windmill Books, An Imprint of Rosen Publishing, 29 East 21st Street, New York, NY 10010

First Edition

Text: Lisa Regan

Illustrations: Moreno Chiacchiera (Beehive Illustration)

Design: Notion Design

Editor: Joe Harris

Assistant editor: Frances Evans

US editor: Joshua Shadowens

Library of Congress Cataloging-in-Publication Data

Regan, Lisa, 1971-
 Riddles at school / by Lisa Regan. -- First edition.
    pages cm -- (Riddle me this!)
 Includes index.
 ISBN 978-1-4777-9173-8 (library binding) -- ISBN 978-1-4777-9174-5 (pbk.) -- ISBN 978-1-4777-9175-2 (6-pack)
 1. Riddles, Juvenile. 2. Students--Humor. 3. School--Humor. I. Title.
 PN6371.5.R4658 2015
 818'.602--dc23
                                    2013048394

Printed in China

SL003660US

CPSIA Compliance Information: Batch #AS4102WM: For Further Information, contact Windmill Books, New York, New York at 1-866-478-0556

Contents

1 Charlie's mom has just gone into his bedroom to wake him for school. She asked him a question, and she knows for sure that he lied when he answered. How can she be so certain?

2 In a math class, the teacher asks: "How may seconds are there in a year?" Amresh says, "Twelve." The teacher thinks for a moment, then says, "Yes, that's correct." How can that be?

3 What does this say?
YYUR
YYUB
ICUR
YY4 me!

4

Answers on page 28

4 The school librarian sets her class a challenge. "Let's say there is a ten-dollar bill hidden in this library. If any of you can find it, then you may keep it as a prize. The money is slotted between pages 57 and 58 of a nonfiction title." Half of the class jump up and start pulling books off the shelves, The other half don't even leave their chairs. Why not?

5 Brutus the dog was born in 5 BC and died exactly ten years later. In what year did he die?

6 Which word has the most letters in it?

5

Answers on page 28

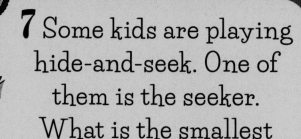

7 Some kids are playing hide-and-seek. One of them is the seeker. What is the smallest number of children hiding if: a girl is hiding to the left of a boy; a boy is hiding to the left of a boy; two boys are hiding to the right of a girl.

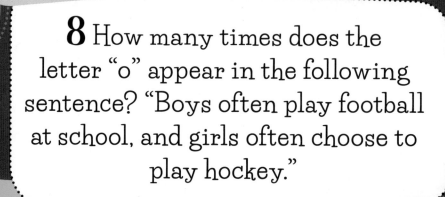

8 How many times does the letter "o" appear in the following sentence? "Boys often play football at school, and girls often choose to play hockey."

9 What am I thinking of? I can take away the whole, and still have some left.

6

Answers on page 28

10 Mystery Word

EACH LINE OF THIS PUZZLE IS A CLUE TO A DIFFERENT LETTER. CAN YOU DISCOVER THE HIDDEN WORD?

My first begins speech but also ends books,

My second's in sees but never in looks.

My third is in nice and also in not,

My fourth is a drink you can make in a pot.

My fifth is the same as my second—
that's handy!

My sixth's in vanilla and bonbon and candy.

My seventh appears in country,
scene, and place,

My eighth's at the end of the tale and the race.

My whole can be written or spoken by any,

But my beginning and end are
forgotten by many.

What am I?

11 What do pixies learn first at school?

7

Answers on page 28

12 A triangle has three sides and a square has four. Why might you say that a bubble has two?

13 If you multiply two by itself twenty times, what answer will you get?

14 Math teacher Mrs. David asked Alex to multiply five numbers together. She read out each, one at a time, but after just one number, he knew the answer. How could that be?

5×6×?=

8

Answers on page 28

15 Can you find a way to make 1,000 with eight "8"s and four plus signs?

16 What number, when written as a word, has its letters in alphabetical order? (For example, it isn't two, since the "o" comes before "t" and "w" in the alphabet.)

17 What is this?
A kind of learning you just don't get at school,
Teachers love it, but pupils think it's cruel,
Your dad or mom might help if they are cool!

9

Answers on page 29

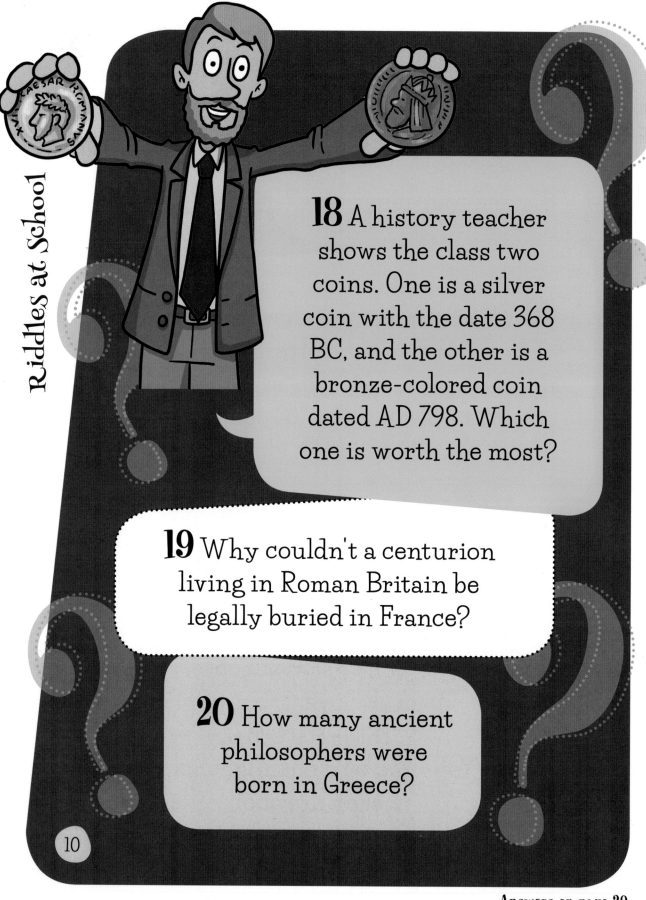

18 A history teacher shows the class two coins. One is a silver coin with the date 368 BC, and the other is a bronze-colored coin dated AD 798. Which one is worth the most?

19 Why couldn't a centurion living in Roman Britain be legally buried in France?

20 How many ancient philosophers were born in Greece?

Answers on page 29

21 What kind of ship would it take to forge an alliance between enemy pirates?

22 No matter how many shields and helmets I smash, you will still own something mightier than me. What am I?

24 Halo of water,
Tongue of wood.
Skin of stone,
For ages I've stood.
What am I?

23 What flies through the air using borrowed feathers?

11

Answers on page 29

25 Recipe:
Take one season.
Add seasoning.
Roll it over and over.
What do you get?

26 I make my mark
On book or card,
But I will break
If you press too hard.

27 What has hands but no
fingers, a face but no eyes,
and moves all the time
without leaving the spot?

12

Answers on page 29

28 Two's company and three's a crowd, so what do four and five make?

29 Mystery Word

EACH LINE OF THIS PUZZLE IS A CLUE TO A DIFFERENT LETTER. CAN YOU DISCOVER THE HIDDEN WORD?

My first is in add but not in subtract,

My second's in picked but isn't in packed.

My third is in over and vacuum and five,

My fourth is in child and bright and alive.

My fifth is in good but is also in bad,

My last is in made but isn't in mad.

My whole is about learning to share things out.

Just ask your math teacher what I'm all about.

13

30 Maisie was learning about adjectives. She asked her English teacher for help. "Miss Stuart, which is correct: My brother chose the bigger half of the cake—or the biggest half of the cake?" What did Miss Stuart say?

31 There are 18 letters in the English alphabet. How can this be?

32 The average English word is five letters long, although it's easy to think of words with more than 10 letters. What is the longest word in the English language?

Answers on page 29

33 What's wrong with a story that's set on a Saturday and Sunday?

34 What Is Missing?

How quickly can you find out what is so unusual about this paragraph? It looks so ordinary that you would think that nothing is wrong with it at all, and in fact, nothing is. But it is unusual. Why? If you study it and think about it, you may find out, but I am not going to assist you in any way. You must do it without coaching. No doubt, if you work at it for long, it will dawn on you. Who knows? Go to work and test your skill!

35 The singular forms of the verb "to be" are: "I am," "you are," and "he, she, or it is." However, can you think of an example where you would be correct in saying, "I is?"

15

Answers on page 30

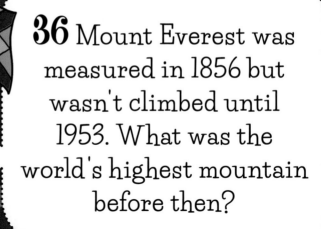

36 Mount Everest was measured in 1856 but wasn't climbed until 1953. What was the world's highest mountain before then?

37 What is the capital of Antarctica?

38 What has four eyes and a mouth, and runs but has no legs?

39 Where is the best place in the USA to learn your multiplication tables?

Answers on page 30

40 I touch the Earth, I touch the sky, But if I touch you, you'll surely die.

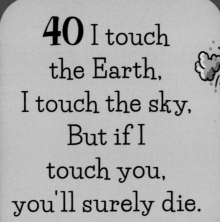

41 My feet stay warm, but my head is cold. No one can move me, I'm just too old.

42 I rest near the shore, never touching the sea, I bring worlds together, yet people cross me.

43 From my mouth belch black clouds and red-hot rain. You could sail upon my river, but your ship would be in flame.

17

44 SPORTS QUIZ

A) Which athlete reaches the top of his or her game and is happy that it's all downhill from there?

B) In which sport do ALL the players go backward?

C) What sport uses a hard white ball and begins with a "T?"

45 What did the baseball glove say to the baseball?

46 Mr. Jennings the PE teacher is one of the 36 percent of teachers in his school who are left-handed. However, he plays racket sports right-handed. Which hand does he use to stir his coffee?

Answers on page 30

47 Mr. Tozer is known for being competitive. One day, he points to himself and then to each member of his class. "We may not be the fastest; we may never win a gold medal; we may never score the most goals. But every one of us has held a world record at some point. What is it?"

48 When the fire bell rang during Miss Smith's lesson, she didn't direct her pupils to any of the fire exits. Why not?

49 I'm easy to catch but hard to hold. You only get me if it's cold.

50 Jimmy has lost his football socks—again. And the light isn't working in the lost-and-found closet—again. There are 17 blue socks and 21 yellow socks in lost-and-found. How many socks must Jimmy grab in the darkness to make sure he gets a matching pair?

19

51 What does a violinist say when she gets her notes wrong?

52 What's this? Thin skin, round sound.

53 This Spanish instrument is also something that a fisherman might do. What is it?

20

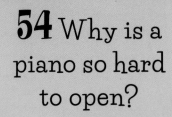

54 Why is a piano so hard to open?

55 Mystery Word

EACH LINE OF THIS PUZZLE IS A CLUE TO A DIFFERENT LETTER. CAN YOU DISCOVER THE HIDDEN WORD?

My first is in forte and twice
in quartet,
My second's in reed but not in duet.
My third is in flute and tuba and drum,
My fourth can be heard at the end
of rhythm.
My fifth is in pitch, piano, and tempo,
My sixth is in volume and twice
in crescendo.
My seventh completes me and
ends instrument;
I'm used to announce an
important event!

21

56 If your science teacher drops a coin into a beaker of water at 20 degrees Celsius, and at the same time, you drop a coin into a beaker of water at 20 degrees Fahrenheit, which coin will sink faster?

57 What has a funny bone but can't laugh?

58 If a doctor is in danger of catching a cold, what is a pilot likely to catch?

Answers on page 31

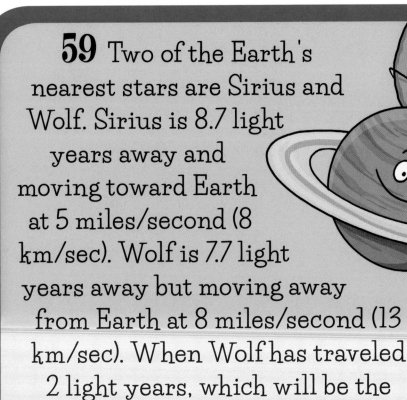

59 Two of the Earth's nearest stars are Sirius and Wolf. Sirius is 8.7 light years away and moving toward Earth at 5 miles/second (8 km/sec). Wolf is 7.7 light years away but moving away from Earth at 8 miles/second (13 km/sec). When Wolf has traveled 2 light years, which will be the nearest star to the Earth?

60 What grows when you feed it but dies when you give it a drink?

61 Which chemical substance is this?
H I J K L M N O

62 When is a blue textbook not a blue textbook?

23

Answers on page 31

63 Mystery Word

EACH LINE OF THIS PUZZLE IS A CLUE TO A DIFFERENT LETTER. CAN YOU DISCOVER THE HIDDEN WORD?

My first ends pharaoh, an Egyptian prince,
My second's in birth and also in since.
My third's in Medusa, Cyclops, and serpent,
My fourth closes feast and banquet and servant.
My next is in Trojan and second in horse,
My sixth is in secret, in crack, and in Morse.
My last is the question that's not who, where, when—
But the "when" in this subject is always "back then."

64 Why were so many Impressionist painters French?

Answers on page 31

65 Some novels start at the end and go backward in time. Can you think of a famous book where August comes before July?

66 Here is a word— six letters it contains. Subtract the last and only twelve remain.

67 What appears once in a minute, twice in a moment, but never in a hundred years?

25

68 Have you heard of a Tom Swifty? It's a sentence that ends in an adverb describing the way Tom is speaking ... but the same adverb also gives the sense of the whole statement. For instance, "I should have written down all the ingredients I need to buy," said Tom listlessly. Can you complete these examples?

"I itch all over, but I won't visit the doctor!" shouted Tom _ _ _ _ ly.

"I know how to make the light work!" explained Tom _ _ _ _ _ _ _ _ _ ly.

"I hate it when it's so cold," grumbled Tom _ _ _ _ _ _ ly.

"I just knocked down all ten pins!" whooped Tom _ _ _ _ _ _ _ _ ly.

26

Answers on page 31

"I came first in my race," admitted Tom _ _ _ _ _ _ _ ly.

"It's more dangerous at the back of the boat," explained Tom _ _ _ _ _ ly.

"We should all take turns on the Ferris wheel," agreed Tom _ _ _ _ ly.

"I twisted my ankle by falling off the curb," said poor Tom _ _ _ _ ly.

27

Answers on page 31

Page 4

1 She asked if he was asleep and he said, "Yes!"

2 There are twelve "seconds" in a year: January 2nd, February 2nd, March 2nd, and so on ...

3 Read it out loud: Too wise you are, too wise you be, I see you are too wise for me!

Page 5

4 Well, they may be lazy or rude, or they may have figured out that there's no way to hide something between pages 57 and 58 of a book, since they are the two sides of the same piece of paper.

5 AD 6. There is no year 0, so when you count, you jump from 1 BC to AD 1.

6 "Mailbox."

Page 6

7 The smallest possible number is three: girl—boy—boy.

8 11—Boys often play football at school, and girls often choose to play hockey.

9 The word "wholesome."

Page 7

10 Sentence.

11 The elfabet.

Page 8

12 A bubble has an inside and an outside.

13 You will always get the answer "four." No matter how many times you attempt it, $2 \times 2 = 4$.

14 The first number was zero, which means it doesn't matter what other numbers are given, the answer will always be zero.

Page 9

15 888 + 88 + 8 + 8 + 8 = 1,000
16 Forty.
17 Homework.

Page 10

18 The one dated AD 798, since the other must be a fake. No one in the year 368 BC could have predicted the dating system we use (they wouldn't know how many years BC it was!).
19 Because he was still alive.
20 None—they were babies when they were born.

Page 11

21 Friendship.
22 A sword, because "the pen is mightier than the sword."
23 An arrow.
24 A castle.

Page 12

25 A somersault: summer + salt.
26 A pencil.
27 A clock.

Page 13

28 4 + 5 = 9.
29 Divide.

Page 14

30 Neither is right—two halves of a cake are equal in size.
31 There are 18 letters in the phrase "the English alphabet."
32 "Language" is the longest word in "the English language."

Answers

Page 15

33 It has a weak end.

34 The whole text does not contain the letter "e," even though it is one of the most common letters in the English language.

35 "'I' is the ninth letter of the alphabet," or "'I' is one of the five vowels."

Page 16

36 It was still Mount Everest—measuring or climbing it didn't change its height.

37 The letter "A."

38 The Mississippi River.

39 Times Square.

Page 17

40 Lightning.

41 A mountain.

42 A bridge.

43 A volcano.

Page 18

44 A) A skier.

B) Tug of war. (In rowing, one person sits facing forward.)

C) Golf. It begins with a tee!

45 "Catch you later!"

46 He really ought to use a spoon.

Page 19

47 Being the youngest person in the whole world.

48 They were doing PE outdoors on the playing field.

49 Your breath.

50 Three socks—at least two of them will be the same color.

Page 20
51 "Fiddlesticks!"
52 A drum.
53 Castanet.

Page 21
54 Because the keys are on the inside.
55 Trumpet.

Page 22
56 The coin in the first beaker. 20 degrees Fahrenheit is below freezing, so the water in the beaker will be frozen solid.
57 A skeleton.
58 A plane.

Page 23
59 The Sun.
60 Fire.
61 Water—H_2O.
62 When it is red (or "read")!

Page 24
63 History.
64 Because they were born in France.

Page 25
65 The dictionary!
66 Dozens.
67 The letter "m."

Page 26
68 Rashly; brightly (or perhaps brilliantly); bitterly (or you could use icily); strikingly; winningly; sternly; fairly; limply (or lamely).

Glossary

adjective (A-jik-tiv) A word that describes a noun (the name of a thing or place).

adverb (AD-vuhrb) A word that describes a verb.

alliance (uh-LY-unts) When people, groups, or nations agree to work together.

centurion (sen-CHUR-ee-un) An officer in the armies of ancient Rome.

crescendo (kruh-SHEN-doh) An increase in the volume or intensity of a piece of music.

enshroud (in-SHROWD) To cover something completely.

forte (FOR-tay) In music, when something is played in a loud or forceful way.

Impressionist (im-PREH-shuh-nist) Relating to a style of art in which the subject is not as important as how the artist uses color and tone.

Further Reading

Burbank, Lizzy. *Jokes for Kids: 299 Funny and Hilarious Clean Jokes for Kids.* North Charleston, SC: CreateSpace Independent Publishing, 2013.

National Geographic Kids. *Just Joking: 300 Hilarious Jokes, Tricky Tongue Twisters, and Ridiculous Riddles.* National Geographic Society, 2012.

Websites

For web resources related to the subject of this book, go to: www.windmillbooks.com/weblinks and select this book's title.

Index